Tgirl.jpg

Tgirl.jpg

Sol Cabrini

ROOF BOOKS
New York

ISBN: 979-8-9896652-3-5
Library of Congress Control Number: 2024931820

Editor: Lonely Christopher
Cover design by Sol Cabrini
Interior design by Deborah Thomas
Author photograph by Robin Michals @robinmichals

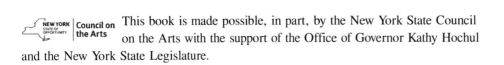 This book is made possible, in part, by the New York State Council on the Arts with the support of the Office of Governor Kathy Hochul and the New York State Legislature.

Roof Books
are published by Segue Foundation
300 Bowery Fl 2
New York, NY 10012
seguefoundation.com

Roof Books
are distributed by
Small Press Distribution
1341 Seventh Street
Berkeley, CA. 94710-1403
800-869-7553 or spdbooks.org

TABLE OF CONTENTS

I WONDER WHAT SIGNS TO LOOK FOR

Today I learned that my home was for me. Today I swept through the notes and needles of my favorite artists with the making of what cannot be possibly found in myself. I stared at the lightbulbs of my broken ideas, shells without a kernel, a furnace without journaling about my blatant adhesion between loving the dead and recovering what's really dead. I thought it was the same thing as being in the middle of something that had never happened before but it wasn't. Instead, the feeling was family. Both familiar and peculiar. I waited seventeen minutes with an amp in hand strapped behind my back for a train to take me anywhere but here. It was heavy. Besides, what am I waiting for? Not much time passes. Sometimes I wonder what's out there outside of waiting for the next thing after the next thing. Am I merely marking time until death in the importance of my existence? Am I looking out at the colors of a passerby shying away from the high of an eye? I'm not surprised at what fades in color. I'm surprised at what evades and portrays yet stays quiet in the rain. Dripping and dropping into the passage of the abstract when discussing thoughts of belonging to the writing that is at hand. When frames emerge, my tongue submerges. I still linger in these kinds of thoughts. Nascent yet nauseous from such deities of desire and worship of language. I still move in other people's summaries. My ideas stray away from the writing. Phantasmagoria.

~_____~

THE SIGNIFICANCE OF LEAVING NO TRACE FOR RECOVERY

When a trace of life dims and departs,
Leaving behind the echo of a heart
The search begins its travels
To come up with your body, to gamble it to rest
A hospital may work to hold your finite frame
While paperwork unfolds a trail of what tomorrow can only name

A sea may sweep your floating verse,
Steeped in the boiling soup of an ocean's storm

A funeral home may fine your open space
And reach out to all who priced your face

A car may be hired, to bear the vacant weight
Through winding entanglement of roads

Where tomorrow's debts lie to the truth that awaits
Where memories etched forevermore
Guts spill over like rivers

Your leftovers left to bear the weight of lease
Or flee the dwelling plea
Your essence echoes through the air as the labor and price handles your share

Attire must be obtained, a garment affair, for the body
Makeup applied with gentle, fragile care of the flesh
A coffin, some kind of vessel handpicked for your silent song

Secure the bend of your voyage for the void to enlarge

A grave, grave, grave… space unveiling the special puzzle of tombstone lore

Never-more known before or ever again

Never-more returnable

Never-more desirable

LAND OF HANDS

Said that you would love me, huh
(boy, please)
I wake when the skies are gray
(fo' real)
I'm hanging with my shadows now
(on god)
I bless up when the stars awake
(no doubt)

My teacher said I'll never leave
(Chicago)
He said I'm just a stupid nigga
(he was racist)

Now I'm in New York, writing figures
Who would figure?
It's been eight years in the mix
Mind yo' business

Bounce with a lean in
Rice with some beans, yeah
Everybody dream, yeah
Cause it's never easy

Now we easy bake, aye
Even tho' we slaves, yeah

Money make a grave what
(money make a grave what)
Money make a grave what
(money make a grave what)

You don't even know who I am
If you catch these hands
It'll land

GARLIC

The moment I forgot
You before I met you
Had the smell of absence
Trinkets of malice
Drenched in garlic of the hour
Our sours stormed the roots
Little culture bared the child
On the grasslands where you could
Not reach them to save
Them from themselves
You gave them rhythm but somehow lost them
In the verse, my dear, we create verse
Soft words behind a thick mask
They come for food and leave with our bodies
So many lost, lost in their wonders.
When they feel you, they kill you
The law that crows its other bird
Wedding children to the ground
No eulogy is as sweet as the last.

BURIED UNDER

On top of leaves
a wooden table
beholds body.
What or who

performing a collaboration
between the living and the dying,
somehow articulating the motion of the undying.
Buried under shards of leaves and twigs,

faces might emerge
as a table holds it
the green leaves tangle with purple flowers.
The ground holds these things
all together the walls around the buried body,
a rectangular corner.
Buried but elevated.
Buried but alive.
Buried but captured.
Buried but seen.
Burial as stage, and stage as re-burial.

THE LIVING ROOM IS FOR THE DEAD

Breaking
Wood
Shaky
Willow
Inky fingers in your mouth
Slithering taste buds
Waking up off with no
Devices
Slippery words on the hot
Metal grate
In wintertime
Who passes who's past
Who passes who's path
Percolating and
Simmering
Is your face somewhere it is not supposed
To be?

RESURFACE

stressed survival
not arrival of life
these breaths we speak
names forgotten and kinetic alike
seamless
unresolved,
rupture,
door of no possibility
dim canvas of casket shells
queer surface celebrates what was, what
is.
who gave you light?

we don't death into
oblivion
the kind that unwinds
morphing your resolve?
no time
for a
normal

T4TELEVISION

If I make it out of this life

I can tell you how to
dream
if I make it out of this house
I might die before I
scream.
don't you ever count to 3

3

or you'll never ever
leave
never let it breathe

you just gotta go to sleep

Demons on my back, I just love to relax
TV talking heads
they don't even know we're dead.

What is death

when you're held by the
law
I'm so appalled

I don't even know I'm lost

Hearing all these voices

do you ever know your
friends?
This ain't how it ends
it just starts up all again.

(If I make it out of this life…)

BRIDE OF FRANKENSTEIN

I am trans. I am building a body to die in. My reflection is re-doubled with this image. I sleep tonight in sight of your insight. The non-simple is already building a body, already speaking in songs, and schisms. It is not an island but ordinary circles of word processors. The shell and the kernel, listening to language. Believe me not to know better. Space filled in order to give you character, teetering to a friendless island. How do you make a bird in the current of air, not know the contrast across the space of being a bird and being in the wind? We don't know where friendship ends. Something happens in the word process. You say yellow. I love you red. Pink bright colors turn to wor(l)ds. I place my morning in your message. Can I hop up on your mind? I hope that you don't mind. Thinking and thanking. I've been on no-mind. You thank another. I can't thank enough.

TGIRL.JPG

Who calls the body of change forth?

When jaded gazes lend themselves to my face

Who knows the auto-bio to be black and graphical?

When worn out faces extend their dismissal

Who demands the study of the bio?

When breast and orifices fold

Phallus

All that has changed is changing in my pal

-ace. Just as,

All that is jaded is de-

faced. Just as,

All that is black is

Punk.

Just as,

All that faded has blurred.

Before I was all
body. Before I was a child of
the screen,
I came from the limits of today's after-image.

Where rivers used to crawl down the steps of rocks as a child of the
ocea-
n. I was cradled by a noise, devoid of a linguis-
tic kiss.
The noise was lost in
time. Fed fables by a
source,
where pixels mark and speak
words. Emitted from the depths of what be-
came distance.
And If I knew I was fallen,
like a leaf in the wind, un-
furled, I would have held my arms
out wide,
without a choice, without control,
where the boundaries of reality and fantasy erode,
and I would have spoken softly to your mourning
blue. I would have whispered to the morn-
ing's fate. And in the silence, I would have
cried a lament.

The rocks that once cradled me
and the rivers that once crawled down their
face are waterways that now flow
through cables.

Words hiding in
words, a sol-
itary walker,
struggling yet yearning to climb out from
monstrosities of the sublime.

THE CAROUSEL OF BORROWED TIME

I have a fleeting sense of world, a half-glimpse of things fading, the faint smell of images lingering like dreams waiting to be obtained, unobtained, or detained. Fresh times—teenage encoded and reloaded, tripping acid near the highway and Lake Michigan. We move through a landscape where genocides genocide in broad daylight, moonlight, and screen-light. You, the weary solver, stare into a mirror and try to solve and settle the cosmic riddle of your own reflection, all while being watched by a gallery full of strangers. This is liberal, us right here in the cosmos of a forgotten sleep. Ambiguous poems become government poems on train stations. This is where the citizen poet finally dies or thrives.

The giant city of chaos and the prairie fields share roads here but they are always days apart. A crack in the Illinois air if nothing at all. I cannot make you understand between the dawn of night and end of day for this all to be clearer. Our world spins like a carousel of colors, sounds, and distant drones but still my hand reaches out to touch the haze of your arm. It's all strange puppetry, the failed project of the human left to poetry.

I wonder if my Midwest smile is borrowed, perhaps from someone back home in Chicago that I've left in a blur for the land of many mountains in the North. I grew up in the heart of the ghetto. I understand it well, the way shadows stretch westward before us, lent not just by daylight and moonlight, but now by the glow of screens. In this timed square, my mother dreams of visiting me, where the storm is a horde of tourists in New York, brewing a cyclone long before the tranquil arrival of the new year.

Maybe our smiles, our sorrows, are borrowed from a kind of library of emotions, each one a volume burrowed in the archive of the soul, a violent collaboration between the State and the flesh. We traverse these dusky edges of consciousness till the symbiotic wheels of time fall off to such a janky interlude. Always there. This is the space between breaths where the world is but a whisper or screen recording on my phone.

The cold of the ocean and the great lakes are always there. The chill of the deep is a constant companion, a reminder of the falling to which one can sink in the search for a shore to call their nightmare. I remember spending some time in Reykjavík and Kópavogur during the wintertime. The sun would bow to the night before my sight could even take hold of its light. We woke up to the night and slept to the night. I remember feeling something similar once on a bus ride to Ohio in the middle of the night to perform my music to a column of strangers.

Once in Berlin, a man yelled in German—slurs directed at a woman for wearing a hijab on a train and then moved on to yell at me. His face became so pink and red. I didn't understand him, I could only understand myself as Black and gender ambiguous in that moment. No-one around us watching did anything. At one point the train had begun to close its door as he stepped out and faced me. As the doors closed, he spat at me. He missed my face. The snot and spit smeared the trains' glass doors in an accident of time. It was almost dark by then. He banged on the doors, but they didn't open. I yelled something back I've since forgotten.

So far away from home—where return is never the same. Never a return, but a turning toward the iteration of anew. Moral of the stories of such night stories: take vitamin D. Soon after, I began watching videos of a comedian describing what he called Midwest Existentialism. Something in it resonated with me, even despite the fact that I come from the Second City. As a Chicago kid, I hardly was able to travel beyond the Midwest area: Gary, Indiana; Jolliet; Naperville; Cincinnati; and more. I still crave Detroit's night sky, where all cornfields lead to Chicago…except when they don't. Reality is awkward as a dream suspended on that edge of awakening. Government poetry enters the commerce of movement, all laid out in plain sight, written from a sense later applied out of that now distant sense, a half-glimpse of things fading through the seascape watched by a gallery full of strangers just near the highway, the train, and the lake.

TRANS(PARENT)OPACITY

Infinitesimale
phantom maybes,
glancing
the glare of an eye with another
hiding.

The still that is
presence.
Handling the limbs of a dismembered memory
All body and still no-body
All color and still dis-color.

How do you occupy a wish with no end?
How do you magnify a gift with no giver?
How do you stop dead middle in the mouth of a translation?
To hold words from sentencing desire to speech.

A WORLD INSIDE YOU

In her reach, the bass unfolds like a midnight tide,
Strung out from the rhythm and the needle
Hanging in the bath with a room of others
They will dance for her when her nose freezes

This is Spiritual
This is Plastic

A snowflake crawling toward the murmur of lava
Instead, it's autumn in the house tonight

The only thing that falls is what leaves
So she doesn't leave, and sways to the heat
So foul their collective stench
Bundled in the porous dilemma between scheme and schema

A complex situation in excess of the burden-
Some re-embodied conditions
To the club looking at the spade

Trans the line once more for her
The active will psyche
A shoulder to cry on
A vibe to pry on
A bump to take on
A body to change from

And she will dance to the same song
Hands and arms long
Dancing years into one song of dolls
All ahead of her selves
Saying, "I miss the times when dolls were just kids' toys"

As she chants for the iron irony side-eyed
Waiting for the drop
Waiting for the kick

Hands tied to the cosmic pop
Tongue spun for water
T-blocked and in the hole
The drum is fun
The bang is on
The spiro will poem
And some will hang them young

I JUST PAID RENT AND I'M SO BROKE AND TRANS

Walk dogs
Sell feet pictures
Look for temp agencies
Sell Adderall
Market your mind
Or become a femboy
Meet demand for trap content
Don't tell people you're a Scorpio
Forget lunch time
Apply
Reject that rejection
Beg
Art your death
No more K
No more M
DM notifications
Till you become one of those trans DJs
In a situation-ship

TOWARD THE HANDS

Today I grew breasts.

I stumbled on them with my hands.

The gravity dances differently.

I feel like an empty television channel

T 4 Television

Black and white dots enter entanglement

Hormonal noise

It is where I am until I transition dead.

BODY AS CONDUIT

                    I lean on the edge of a transi-
              tion. Where my conduit of pleasure to
         change body

Is molded by the abyssal shape of my own
hands.

                         The edge asks me to take a stand.
                            But if I rise I
                            fall. The fall flies
                                Black
                         only my lean fed by loss of
                         breath. I channel the edge
                         without pain. For limits with-
                                out a body.
                         I fold in floral wonders of smells gone
                         astray bleeding into the bed of an
                                ocean's creases
                         I'm held at an an-
                    gle my hands hold the edge as if it could be
                                grounded
                         to an ephemeral deep dive

SO I

Found my body

        Caved into obscureness

                Onto the background

In a distance

                I found it in other bodies

I lost it when no-body was around
There was no vessel that could provide its return
Performing a calamity of re-collection
When skin can't fathom a color of absence

BODYBUILDING

usefulness of a thing

determines a use-value.

but this usefulness

does not dangle in mid-

air.

it's conditioned by phys-

ical chattels of the raw,

with no existence apart from this law.

.JPG

we know lessons about loss   the kind that remind us of our world to gain

the kind that maneuvers the body to dance   with change
we know the loss to be transferred   the kind that re-forms in a formless world

the kind that re-works harm that form has marked   we know the dance
at the level of the feel
             the tech is bio   the loss is hack-in
away at the former   away at the purloined kiss

from the level to the flesh
to the waters in the chest
              we know about alteration
opening   of the wound of life again
all these spiritual retrials for the gravel of rebirth   spaced in the chalice
             of a dialogue unlike any other word

the zone of politics and amorousness
             strung by the chord of the blood pumping
          commerce to the air of the breaths we try to share

we know lessons about everyday trans-formation
         the kind of trans-sublimation

             unmaking the re-making

we don't outlast it   we don't surpass it   we don't transcend it   we don't

reprimand it   we carry it together willingly   all over to the ground

                                                                                          watching

over each other

DO RE ME

How could I have found the busted speakers buzzing between the backdrop of dissimilar chemistry anywhere but you? You make the conceptual practice and ask like Iverson, "What is practice?" You tell me tales of grand-composure. And when I'm heavy headed, you bathe me in your humming. I often contemplate what I cannot face. I've spent my hours in the summers of young ashtrays fretted by the impacts of strings and delirium progressing along the necks of guitars, off-beat soon to be dead speakers, and unwarranted displacements of what I first knew to be real. There must be something between the theatrics of numerous nerves percolating a curve in my body and the reverb from the acoustics of your soul's otherworldly tremolo. Maybe it's an ephemeral emerald inter-vowel. I could listen to your voice from every angle that would fabricate what defines a day to end. Because all I know that keeps arising from those dark brown crystals of pupils hugging the array of shared light, is the kind of travel which unravels the finite to be more possible, enabling me to say, you make me feel more possible, how is that possible?

AN INDEX FOR GLISSANT

Poetics—the mishandling of all things language

Repetitions—the tone of poetry slipping

Imaginary—the home of exile's wishes and memory

Exile—astral astray, fluctuating for a relation it escapes

Relation—always in motion

Open—free to all and none

Echo—Always already tracing something lost, abyssal, and new

[NO 1.] WHERE [NO 2.] DID YOU [NO 3.] COME FROM AGAIN?

Where

I have no outfit for the tender bliss that we share
for it is not a show to be put on, but a feeling that we wear and if the shackles that bind us
give you flight
then I will be your crater through the spaces of all nights

A bowl for your impact
so that when you land
on land I can find
where you're
confined

Because when a strand of your sentiment is on the edge of my
tongue I will hold it gently and weave it into a song that can
never be unsung

Did You

So do not breathe if bitterness causes you to
shutter, do not reach if the touch causes you
to flutter

All things are porous, all things stray
and in the wind that bends the clocks of ticks, we find our way

playing the drums on skin, with symbiotic cymbals clashing
eating a life just a corner away, but never thrashing
for in the real world's parasite, we dream with open organs of sight

And see the green in the darkness, the light in
the lies of music's ticks and turns
nourishment with a doubling elocution drawn from the
branches of your throat
let's speak dissent, for someone may have said that gods do not hear a poet's prayer

Nor for their ears to bear
where shadows dance and colors ignite young odor

Persist, persist,
persist…. like this,
as they linger in the spaces between our dreams

Adjourning our thoughts, and unraveling
our seams in a sea of ideas,
in a world that spins as it does seem

In the laughter of a child, the warmth of the
sun, in the gentle embrace of a love in the air

In a world that's both strange and familiar, where we begin
where we've been beyond repair
in the silence of the mind, in the chaos of the free
in the cracks of our imperfections, in the scars of our past

Oh how our souls twirl to the chorus of the
free, a new note played, a path laid

To see it in the small things, in the everyday
in the kindness of strangers, in the words that we say

Come from Again?

Sometimes the music falls out of tune
and we find ourselves lost, feeling marooned
but even in those moments, maroon can be a symphony in the air

A cosmic verse everyone and everything disputes as being free or fleeing
so if our bondage leads to your light
I'll be your crater in the midst of the night

If I have no outfit to breathe your tenderness
I'll be the feeling of something harsh wearing off
snowflakes falling like delicate lace
a reminder of something that is or was

In the spaces between notes
the rustle of leaves and crunch of snow
beneath the feet marching to a church

A flicker stumbling upon its own self-por-
trait, impressions left on the bruises of a
body tumbling a formidable fumble
falling out into the morning light

Because when a strand of your sentiment is on the edge of my tongue's immutable hunger

I will hold it young as only the old can

Sung a bowl from your impact
non-locatable sentiments
intimacy rushing ever so clear into me celestial vapor
making an impression on me
Where did you
come from again?

MIDWEST EXISTENTIALISM

I been on no mind
Can I hop up on yo mind
I hope that you don't mind
If we hang around till 5
The weather treats you good
The sun on you is awesome
I wish that I could blossom to the stature of your talking
I'm usually always late but I'd bring some charms to date
Our fate's fini - tude
But its feel like endless inter - ludes
Always in-between
The light is dim
The bite is slim
To each her own
I be feeling like I'm gone
We can stay awake for days
Promise that this ain't a phase
I know that I can give
And that's all that I can give
Can you hold me down
When I crave flight
Tripping though these sounds like a grave sight?

24

written by solei

Say you're around when you know you're out of reach
You want to love when you know no one can teach you
The lesson goes that I'm only here to please
Letting go just to learn not two beliefs

Don't want it all
Just want something for me too
Can't let it go cause I know just what you mean
To me

Long as you know
Wherever you go
Long as you know
Wherever you go
Long as you know
Colors don't bite they can only heal
You can only fall when you're off the ground
Colors don't bite they can only heal
You can only fall when you're off the ground
Like they told you
When there's no truth
But to search through

A colored film
If it's too deep you can only die
If you hold on you can only bruise
If it ain't real you can only bleed

42nd

Projects tore up
Gangsters don't grow up
I never had to throw up
I'm rapping like my fro's back
I'm broke like the world view
But I still love you
Death of the cool
Turn a jack to a sunroof

I used to be nostalgic
Now I'm just around, bitch
Catch me on a rhombus
Opposites acute means I equal what I shoot, bitch
Ever seen the world in a poem? In a loose fit

That's why I don't talk no mo'
How many tabs did I take just to last this

I used to pop xannies to flo
That's why I can't feel you anymo'

We used to sip molly in cup
Days turn to years now what's up
I haven't been home in a minute

I gave moreee than I can go give no more
I lived in a potluck queer interval
I never knew that this world kill my soul
I wasn't innocent but I did have hope

This is for my niggas outside all winter
This is for my aunties outside cooking dinner
This is for my grannys' out styling Anna Wintour
I wrote this for my mommas
I wrote this for my brothers

This ain't
What you think is
I'mma Chicago kid
I gotta rhyme like this

Backpack raps at a time like this
Mr. president can you catch these hands
From a transb(ian)eing
I mean I'm just saying
Jokes on you we still alive
But still deprived
They want us dead but at work
So we look to the divine
When we killed by 12

My skin is a curfew
My flesh is a virtue
I grew from the cookouts
The south is en route

The BBQ make ya wanna mild the sauce out
To Englewood err body get they feet out
Old heads house heads two stepping to Muuuuuurda She Wrote
We gotta up turn up the soul

BABY

I used to bike from 42nd
To Belmont had all these lovers
To Humboldt Park
With no dollars on me
My real mom like where you
Going baby
Well, these drugs used to be my only baby

Lake Michigan when I'm going crazy
Can't miss me again with these fading words
I used to want to leave this world

Lonely life
Fold me twice
So precise
The way I like
I'm on my yeah
Hopping around
Holding it down
Came for my dreams
Aye

Ducking them bullets
But hoping they pull it
I'm open and broken to lean mean

I seen them things beam bleed
I had them souls leave lanes (lanes)
I had my rouge feet breathe
Running from opps
Running from cops
Running the block
Hoping to pop
My   head   off

So I had to head off

LONGING FOR

In your vicinity of touch

I cling, I clutch, and speak as

such, in your enemy of lost

I grieve, I sleep, I keep

out of the empty sealed can-

dle, in the cradle of fire

where an open lid

seeps into the distance that hisses

hold me closer because going is not yet gone

kiss me wholesome because half is a deca-

dent song

WONDER TO WANDER

Engraved silhouettes in neon lights
Rhymed and dipped
In the polar compass of nowhere
Intensifying somewhere
So many lost yet still surviving
Unresolvable group sex
In each other's body modifications
Slanting the muse of you amused
In the whirl of changing ways
Is it your words I'm twisting
Felt in the straddle of a shock
Theres countless ways
To let old loves die
I sighed at your last message
Thought we were syncing,
Then you changed the bars
The muse of your music thrifted
Inharmonic melancholia
The bruise of your museum
I'm not who I was, not after a few
Counting moments with you

LETTER RAIN

I
ache, I bite my
tongue
I
squirm
I la-
ment
I whisper your name.
None of us are sim-
ple it all pours down
on me
I dialogue the turns and quotes of you
I relearn my heart of
you I wish a return of
you makes me want to
break up with the
world
I decline with time of
you I impulse and decide none
of you
I am not sure if I'm the person of
you I whither to the sound
of you
I pain and feel it to close for you

IN OF IT AND BUT FROM IT

I'm all in love
Plucked out from my hidden burrows

Sipped onto the seams of lips
At a deep distance from my sorrows

Quenched moment to moment
Held in a nexus

Prowling my weight out of the canvas I'm all
Drenched while percolating

I look across the distance of the hollow
Tunnels

Once carved in my arms

I see the trinkets of Ghost wonder
Inside the emptiness I once called home

There's a market just above their
Cornerstones I'm not buying it anymore

I'm off the grounds of such graveyards
I'm all in love and those lips
Are all the above

YOU'RE NO LONGER IN PAIN

There's a moment when you start to sing.
Not only out of the mouth but through that dance of the body
In spaces compiled of noise
Pedestrian onlookers
Those marks of movements
Carving and indexing something into you
Where you meet the image with the imagined
Just as the sonic feeds the atmosphere.
I tried reaching you on a call but the line was busy
Suddenly bubbles started blowing across your face
And you noticed, briefly excited
It made you remember some distant child

LAVI DISTANS

Toudunkou	All at once
Un momen arivé	A moment arrives
Toudunkou	All at once
Li chimbo sô rèv	It holds one's dream
Toudunkou	All at once
Tremblé lamou tou	Trembles all love
Toudunkou	All at once
Réyinnyon enkò	Gathering again
Toudunkou	All at once
Un boté vid	An empty beauty
Toudunkou	All at once
A tô kœr	To your heart

LEVELS OF WACKER DRIVE

Walking in the world t'day / Can't ease or stop / I was lost on lower Wacker / Where da trees don't talk / Had to trip on a heart joke / Everybody want to smoke / Till they get smoked / I wasn't living on reggie / I was living on fuk me / Before you could ever love me

I'on do flowers in towers / Cut my throat in this hour / When does it all feel so sour? / And you can't cope with some power? / When they love to abandon you dire / I never can fan up the fire / I always alone when I'm tired / I write when I'm full of the desire / My mind is an open multiplier / How many thoughts do I have to aspire to / Just say I'm (un)like you

I wonder how my dreams used to live in a layup / Make it outta the hood just to make another system / Living in an apparatus of a rhythm / I wonder how the world looked outside before I / Was thrown in its prism (prison) / Or grown in it to be risen

I BEEN ON / LEAVE ME / TILL I WRITE IT IN POEM

Yeah, I did you wrong
But did you die?

Money ain't ya maker
But it will definitely make ya

Profit off your cables
Tethered through your body

Profit off your family

Operate your labor

Murder all yo' grannies
And them daddies too

But that's a prerequisite

Just to make a life
Yeah, that's a pre-recording

Friends make it worth it
But worth ain't a purpose
We just touch the surface
Because real love makes us nervous

I love you in most the impossible

Way

When there's no longer any possible

Day

NOT EAZY

I don't look any more foolish
Than the next person you see
I don't look any more foolish
Than the next person you see

You see
You see

What I'm saying is easy
I love with no remorse

No regrets
Choke my neck
I leave the beat
On MIA
Damn I say
Can I say

Ability ain't signature
Be mature

Used to rap on pizza from Lil Caesars
Now my jaws are jeepers creepers
I'm stalking for your allegiance

To my compromised demons
I'm feeding on the top
When my pain is at the bottom

Walking through Gotham autumn
Concrete New Yorker problem

The train is late

                                                                        Wait

                                                                I'm 25 away
                                                                        Wait

                                I'm an hour away
                        Around the corner for today
                                                        I'll meet you on the way
                                                                        Wait

I'll be there in a second
This line ain't running either

                                                                I gotta take uh shuttle
                                                                        Wait

                        It's a date?

ALMOST HAPPY WITH IT

With all these other moves you tell me to relax
If you were a track star, you would say we're finished

If you were a rider well, I'd be your lane
I don't date detectives but I can be your clue
But you be like a pilot when you say you taking off

You say that I'm soft, well
I think that your right, yeah
I been searching heights for everything you like
Cause if you were a river, well I'd like to be your bank
Get you something pricey

I could be your proxy
Put you on the web like
Spiderman in Mile's life

Why you gotta mock me
I can't even pose for you

Say you're doing well
When I'm telling you to feel for us
Damn I think I fell for us
Now I gotta run, Forrest

I be seeking nuns for ya
Praying for them lungs for ya
Breath is like ensemble
Singing in them dark tunnels

Taught me how the love life
Picked me and ground me
But I can't even time out

I just want your lips like
All up on my timetable
Plan it out then drop me

I can't say I'm fine but I know that I'm fine
I know you see the signs
So
Hit my line offline
Hit my line offline
Hit my line offline
Running out of time

SEXY WITH ABSTRACTION

I want to feel sexy; I want to feel like my body loves me. Who is this 'me' though? 'Me' who occupies a language developed for the body, may that 'me' be the enunciation driven between those ordinary occurrences of doubt put into reverse. I want to then ripple this face with a fading gesture just near that window of a feeling unfamiliar to sexy with abstraction. I cannot recall how many times I've heard the not-knowing touch my leg, pull at my throat, and scope in a new thought. Instead, I have temporal nightmares with sexy. Am I haunted by my soul? The spirit that claims to occupy my vehicle of desire?

BEMOANED MOON

A hand saunters through the alley
A passage falls through its paw
To be handled
A figure reappears

A birthplace patrols in its valley

A cause for concern becomes relearned
To be out there in the eyes of a cosmos
The not leaving it ahead
Where scenes fall off its thread.

We dimmer the handles' floral appearance
Misled into saying, "Let me feel it."
Another voice responding, "It's in the doing of my own feeling, how could you ever—k,"
To which another voice quickly chimed in,
"I know because…. something was shared."
The conversation ends at the noise.

The hallway light flickers silently
And then a "light bulb went up"
Like a phrase rephrasing keys, cranks, and buttons.

A dead innovation

All in my head and the head before your head

To keep it beyond reach of the others, might be to keep it so close to you.
To be out there so blue in the eyes of a cosmos.
Carve out my stomach
Leave my mouth to wonder

Where my organs stop singing and rhyming

As you read along the misty breeze like so many others in a dream.

MOONSET

A passage in the frame of a heart blisters at night
it begins to spread out into threads of time
                                   where chambers have smelt like whimsical seasons
where there is now no more bridges to tie the crowd of hearts over these creases.
Wedges are thrown
                                   Everyday disfigurations of reason are shown
reopening wounded noise
                                   once more again
prying out without any resolutions of truths
                                   looking automated to work out some more ruckus
the people are trying to twist their body in this world again
                                   absurdly smiling
                                   in the aisle of such awaiting
that will never be again.
Is this how it feels to be a phantom in the daylight's moonset?
Mundane whispers from chapped lips
                                   shadows hung over the decision-making process
where   of serenity become dilemmas of abstraction
                                   buzzing the news of new truths
in a distance a woman harbors over to the next person beside her in deep interlocked
                                   stares.
The next person exchanges a final glare
                                   moving out of sight by a hair
from a collision in the busy traffic of despair
                                   the city steps become flatting
                                   passages, extensive concrete
                                   all laid out

amongst the rounds of the ground

                    beneath them.

Out of the hurdle of another passerby

      the sky light recedes from its descendants

creeping back into the attic of the city's axis

                    just as the night begins to host a party of four at the

                    local travesty.

Whatever breath is shared here

                    on these grounds

motivates the motions of affairs to decay

                    at the plight of a person

                    becoming a person of worth.

Whatever promise is said by these animals of worth

premised on the bearer of uncertainty.

                    Submerges,

                    ushering forth a caricature

                    seeping out of the onlooker's blurry perception.

                    Poor riddance to those street sweet lovers hovering

                    amongst the changing genders of conditional

                    speech

Poor riddance to those old laughters

colored brown amongst their gone brownstones.

Jagged four-to-six-legged walkers are opening an oat milk café

                    in the interior intolerant sector of a historical

                    district renamed, remade, reborn for another

                    name, we will not name

justice is hung here

right above everyone's heads

                              out of reach.

BAY OF SEALS BLUE

I miss you
As if my heart could be split yet whole in two
I wanted you to save me
As if my heart could be a ship adrift
I dye my ideas of you
As if my heart could be the cloak of your color
Bleeding rivers
A masterpiece in shades of blues
Vivid and true
Labyrinth obtuse
Straddling with what's the use
Calling the ketamine's goose
A grace to your fateful move
I'm all out of my heart
As if the pattern could hold
This poem to your palm
This longing to your chest
As if the pattern could have sold
The gravity that stands
On all the details of your mark making
Me remake the maze to my gut
This feeling that cannot keep up
As if the narcotic tasted of a choral prayer
The abrupt reality of this missing message
All laid out with batted organs of sight
Replaying an image throughout the night

A MONTH

For you to have a path
beside the joys of your return
in the change of the day.

For the intangible essence of your breath
to wonder, ponder, and meander your return
in the splices of time.

The joy of your return is a promise felt beside
the sense of your voice
all splayed out.

How will I?
When can I?

THANK YOU

First word of gratitude

The phone that doesn't ring

Something I can't put on hold

This is the way I think you

The storm that never reigns over the city

Ordinary delusions

It knows it has impulses

Losing and regaining touch

Does trauma train life?

Does it drive what it teaches?

What are edges of a life's composition?

Feeding the play with music

Arriving to speak.

Curated and willing

Sources of sounds reminding the word distance

A shape I cannot make out with a no-idea at the rear of

                    romance. Void of thinking one-

                    self. unjoined

Does sound reach for that kind of pi(e)ace of distant

                    rhythm, un-rhythmning repairs

                    the

sound to

prepare the music for its fading lights, lights fading, unfading.

I'm always out of time

Time out of always,
looping, un-looping,

as replay inherits another kind, each on the

brink of that

which has no pattern. Displacement feeds

                    collaboration.

Looking out for the other in the distant fu-
                              ture, asking

                              without the

                              phone ringing not ringing.

The music

                              the music

                              thank you for listening.

CALL DROPS

Today it'll rain all day.
Can you sleep in and
Out?

I missed your call
But I'll call back—
Whenever the call is delayed and drops to the ground or breaks up

I also have an umbrella for that second calling ground
A rainy day at the distance of all days.

VANE?

You make rhythm and blues sound mad
Intonations fracture and amplify   …
You make those sweet sweet songs scream and   …
A peak is put under erasure
We meet where the melody aches
So much so that you make me unable to rhyme
Unable to poem in a frame of mind
The underlying meaning of a peak out of frame then becomes
The unpredictable return of ……………..… to gain.

CITY OF HEART

I brought my heart to this city of art
Had friends, loved ones torn apart
I try to love like I'm the only above none
Got sheet covers from ex-lovers
Who can't love us

My hangover like makeover makeup
I'm living in the limits if it's a breakup
Cause I use to play pick up

Hooping in the alley
Homegrown valleys
Crates were the baskets

I dreamt on ad-lib
I wrote it into madness
Days get to passing
I'm talking like its average
But it's just nostalgic
Nothings everlasting

Came from a roof that collapsed
On my face

I'on need face
But I give if its fate

Gotta give it up regardless
You know we all broken art-ists
That's what art-is
What's already there shifted
But then that delusion comes back around
and tells you you gift-it

TALKING TO YOU IS LIKE OPENING A WOUND

The kind that shows its insides too long

The scruff fallen onto an exhale

Of never reliving the mask of your face

Remade memory

A wipe out that just destroys

And relies on my labor

An abrasion of puncture

A stab with a slash that grazes and rips up my breathing

GIVENESS

I can't give it to you rough
When I give in to you hard

I can't utter all your grace
When I give in to your fate
Trinkets of tales fall deep on your breathing
Sometimes I feel it's only good when the grace escapes
And what we are left with

Are the snuggles of the day
At the dawn of boiling a bowl from the sky
Underneath your eye

LINE BREAK

Welcome to the line

Cue places me as it replaces me.

I'm beside myself

Disassociating into the sea of summers.

There's always another line to wait in. We stood in lines in school.

The line is always on

Bottom line is that you had to learn this about line

But when I'm open I'm held with no flooring

Like a floral animation of a garden spread out across different sea levels

I wake up to this swirl of thoughts unaligned

Rising and riding the tide of midnight into the midday

Saying to myself the unsayable.

I wait in the line from the club to the grocery store or to the hospital.

I imagine conversations.

Conversations that have never happened. I desire and I do not desire.

These conversations are out of line. I wonder what that's all about.

When doing lines of drugs, I worry that I'm waiting in line to die.

My rehearsal for life collapses into the moment of the unanticipated

Miraculous speechless tunes of the unrehearsable.

I want to fade into that rounded void

Between knowing and learning

Screaming at the thickness of the bass in my voice.

What do I learn that I cannot possibly know?

Knowing something is what I was taught provides relief.

But can I feel relieved without a confirmation of ever having known it?

Thoughts cease to stutter in my mind or align

When I have no words for my lines of thoughts is when I feel that anything might be possible.

LEFTOVER

I slept in a dark room for three years. Once without a roof above my head where the flood had kicked in. I have untitled sketches about when I'm obviously blue, in a city of moves and hand-held rent. I city the groove in lieu of events. I'm only young as I can grow. Already as old as I can die. I'm only as trans as I will ever know. It's funny because in a poem it all becomes something else, once the poet mentions the other outside of them, by way of the pronoun you.

But what about the impressions left inside of me…
Don't those marks of the outside left inside of me require some listening to?
These are the meditations.

I thought that ordinary delusions were a secluded area of belief
Now I realize it's what you make of it.
Practical and imaginative are far more fragile than the distinctions appear.

I'm always thinking like this…
I'm always thinking like this…
Like this…

So, if I told you a story…
What would be your discretion
And If I spoke you
Would you feel some attachment
Would you love me in the aftermath?

BLURRING THE VERB

A narrow thorough
Fold in disguise
With complete disregard
To be not superficial or partial
A space of thought under the duress of a thing
A system intrinsic to being apparent
Apparently folded such disguise
A narrow mirror of what is truly outside
What hides behind us also means what falls before us
In other words, a thorough focus is only in front
Insofar as the non-focus blurs.
A line of sight does not see a person from behind
But rather this behind is consequential
To what will lie before us
Ability in a system of regard and disregard
Disguises the disabilities that give fuel to its space of thought.
Absence performs rhythm in all sorts of untimely ways.
Under this duress, abilities to enslave, rehabilitate, and redistribute under and over-
Tones/terms by which those abilities are being put to focus, but what's seemingly outside
Is much greater than the narrow establishment of conceptualization.

ARCHIE SHEPP IN THE CITY

Brooklyn, 7:15 PM

Jazz quenches the schizophrenic's antennas. Reaching and withholding what's shared between the beholder and the instrument, collapsing the puppeteer and the puppet into the dance of music as an event. Spirit that did not cross my mind but rushed forward. Archie is playing. They all are playing. Reading is playing with the dead and the living. They don't just jam, they glide across the bread and butter of an audience's attentiveness. If they hook you in you never get out, only further into their aftersound. Those jazz players have left an impression on you like micro details carving out the expression of a door's architecture. You turn the knob till it locks itself inside you, like a poem stopped halfway dead. Suddenly the closing preludes your finiteness. An instrument of life is what you are. A being of the moment is what you want but the past just snuffs that moment right before your eyes. Smile child. Heed the decoration of keys and dialogues to your high. Archie's grandma was born during slavery.

JAZZ BONE DRILL

Chrome on chrome   Chrome on chrome
Gotta roam on Rome Gotta roam on Rome
I edit like I exchange ongoing carbon come
An ex gone ghost   An ex gone ghost
I flex on both   I flex on both
I'm always on the low I'm always on the low
My mind is a boat   My mind is a boat

Niggas wanna joke
I just wanna cope
Niggas wanna cop
Till they see the cops
She say wanna W.A.P.
I just ate h'a whopper
I just gotta rock
I'on do em rocks
I'm from the ol' Chi
Where they shoot with no eye
Crosshair niggas
Wanna jazz bone drill
Do it for a thrill
Till they pass on ill
I just had to live it till I knew that I could pivot
We was 6–7

On dat do you bang?
Watchu thank?
You smiling
Raise money for ya casket
Yo mother
       Yo brother
              Yo uncle
                    Yo sister
                         Yo cousin
                              Yo auntie
                                 You cussin'
                                      You dead cause yo being is ahead
                                      You dead cause of existential dread
                                      You dead cause the State is always there
                                      You dead cause the bullet's unaware

My mind is a **Moat**mind is a **Moat**mind is a **Moat**mind is a **Moat**mind is a **Moat**mind is a boat
My mind is a **Moat**mind is a **Moat**mind is a **Moat**mind is a **Moat**mind is a **Moat**mind is a boat
My mind is a **Moat**mind is a **Moat**mind is a **Moat**mind is a **Moat**mind is a **Moat**mind is a boat
My mind is a **Moat**mind is a **Moat**mind is a **Moat**mind is a **Moat**mind is a **Moat**mind is a boat
My mind is a **Moat**mind is a **Moat**mind is a **Moat**mind is a **Moat**mind is a **Moat**mind is a boat
My mind is a **Moat**mind is a **Moat**mind is a **Moat**mind is a **Moat**mind is a **Moat**mind is a boat
My mind is a **Moat**mind is a **Moat**mind is a **Moat**mind is a **Moat**mind is a **Moat**mind is a boat
My mind is a **Moat**mind is a **Moat**mind is a **Moat**mind is a **Moat**mind is a **Moat**mind is a boat
My mind is a **Moat**mind is a **Moat**mind is a **Moat**mind is a **Moat**mind is a **Moat**mind is a boat
My mind is a **Moat**mind is a **Moat**mind is a **Moat**mind is a **Moat**mind is a **Moat**mind is a boat
My mind is a **Moat**mind is a **Moat**mind is a **Moat**mind is a **Moat**mind is a **Moat**mind is a boat

FEVER

My surface has no ports.

No place to tie your boats.

I welcome only my sharks.

Only the parts that navigate with edges.

Only the parts that navigate
with edges.

MUNDANE BARRETTES

And then there's that orbit of misery and mystery

Beautiful mistakes of a promise gone astray

Social pathways tip-toeing into delicate curves

Disturbing the elegance of elders trekking into the muddy waters of a kiss or a hug

The mystique becomes a mistake

That lacerates itself to a rhythm

Wrapped up in the scattered domains of water without a cup to shape its bluff

All collapsed onto the levies

The mystique becomes musical

With old faces in the sea

Not having the plea to promise the same path of reach

We feed the galactic doves of the young here

We reach into that unknown

From New Orleans or Brookhaven to Chicago

Onto the fruit held by older hands dangling our blood splattered banner

To usurp a labyrinth of stars

From the curls of our braids to the curls of a hurricane

Elder hands hold onto the knots and kinks of creation

Our hair stands on this premise of abstraction

We don't just waste away to pass here

With Grandma's arms outstretched and braiding

With a hymn on a yam for the grim reaping harvest

Just the near kitchen of Cabrini Green

Even with breath gone faint

With water without one cup to shape the dark flux

We influx the redux

Starve out what's lost

Cook those fragments from dust

Braid those barrettes to communion

Summoning nothing out of nothing

To no one thing

INHALE ME

Me so Mississippi
Kiss me tall

With a scent whose space stenches back
To inhale me into a doll

A fly on the wall
If nothing at all

Because there's no sizzle here
Without the grit of a riddle's jaw

CABRINI HYMNS

With all those liquids descending from the eye
Edging towards the tear of the sky
Recording those modes of ruckus
From the elevator to the staircase
To the collaboration between piss, mildew, and dreams

At every angle, the isolated block is a common project
We honed its dis-symmetry
Rolled up the dice on the face of doom
Cooked up gumbo before the funeral
Grilled those migratory phantoms to juke
And fed our spirits some soul
In order to raise our kids in a home
On top of another home
In those black skyscrapers

Where we wondered on its beat with cheap ragged clothes and torn up soles
Inside the seat of the feet running here and there
Our New Orleans heat sizzled up and down Sedgwick Street
Going nowhere but anywhere around the block of our Chicago heart

MY HUMBLE WAVS

I just live it when I don't have no guidance
I'm talking days when you looking for no one to free you
My mother working in the Matrix
I just to hope to see her
I come from gravestones
Milestones
Slave songs

I come from Midwest
Mild sauce
Patience

FOR COZY BLACK FOLKS

Spiral into oblivion light years
How far is near
How close is far
Sun ray between all desire
Gravity in the sea of wonder
Swallowed in tongues of testimony
Who live by hands coated similar
Grabbing each-other's rhythm-and-flesh
To song that is made to sing-again
Practice not the game, not the death rain,
Instead promise the day of laying hands
On cozy ashtrays

intoxi-catering-services

Between heatwaves of seas seeping between the knees
And the age of raining legs dangled acrosssssssss the
black abstract

WINDING WOUND

Remaining visions, disposed Black summer, imprinted apparatus.

I have
cruel visions,
The stigma warmth creates, scars cannot.

Imprinted shoreline, swirled Black doorways, cotton illusion.

A
cruel tear,
consequential ruptures that undid summers, taste indigestion.

THE CAMERA MAN SAID LET THERE BE LIGHT

Color graduations
Color gradations
Toxicity and heroisms
On camera
Obliterated bodies still at work
Going live
Language games of cinema
We are the feeling of matter
The shadow of flesh in the soul
Flight for your reverence I know

FREE

Free. Tyshawn.
Free. Dennis.
Free. Sherry.
Free. Darin.
Free. Johnathan.
Free. Rix.
Free. Denzel.
Free. Chronos.
Free. Thana.
Free. Nefertiti.
Free. Monte-Quarlo.
Free. Erin.
Dead or Alive. Free.

AN ANTAGONISM WAS PRE-RECORDED

Blood did not

Could not

Life was not

Life became not only for

Family could be out stripped at any moment

Cannot be put back together

An antagonism was pre-recorded

BAD POETRY

I'd rather eat the dust or let myself simmer
on the train of er-
rors with those woods out at
the steak all coated in oblique
blues jazzing my unclenched
cool tapping and tipping my
being
I keep at the wake just to dust this
tremor holding my hands on the
pockets of eyes
darting their shins, cheeks in the grin shape of a
lime with their sour oozing hands out
grasping I'm training these errors for mir-
rors of thorns with each step down that
avenue of gratitude
beside the next mind that
hides a throw within the
thrown
where your question then grows
and grows till it has grown because
this is where you ask, "How to keep
alive when the live is not I," wad-
dling past tenses
I try to hold those
things but the tremors of endings will fold
my spring
into bad po-

etry, that's the lov-
ers ring
all thrown up in each
other that's the fly that
falls that's the wrinkle
who calls
my temperature is to bare this glare at a distance

TICKING COLORS

Blood thickens

clots bring breakage

to a shriveled kiss

from the freezing cracks hum-

ming between lips. There's

nothing till there's something

we pass it, jazz it, and still can-

not outlast it. These bare bones

of home.

MANY MEANY MEANS

The words be misshaped bundled and humbled, fumbled and mumbled
Off aunts and uncles, take the tunnel of chuckles
Chipped in troubles of doubles
Ditching and
Flinching muzzles
Held in a tussle of subtle
Repercussive beats of tonsils
Books of long-used stand-still read in the beds of housing
The beings of speaking monsters daring to shout I in the found feel of withheld
Means of chanting
The words be mis-worded
Gargled and parted in both ways startled in columns of what's sane
Or what one's saying
They will write it and rewrite it if they cannot say it ranting
The family of means and words of dreams

SO THIS IS A POEM ABOUT

This is a poem about

                                So I wrote this when

The title of this poem is

                                So I made this when

This is something I've been

                                So I've been working on

This is called

                                So I've been meaning to share

These are from

                                So I've been looking at

This took me a

                                So this piece came

This an homage to

                So I had this idea

If people can read poetry in confusion, can we do that with other lines of thought? After I arrived at the lake of passion, the devotion to the services and the servers from bouncers to coat checkers, at the club, I slip away from any word or conversation I have heard previously. I join a party of five and many more upstairs for the tranquil yet catatonic intermission of substance. Friendships pick up where we leave them. Days ago do not end. We come and go, not as we please, but by way of the different people who put the club together night and day. The freedom they give us, lives without us, and extends beyond.

In the intermission of meeting again, our nostrils spun to the muted record that was below the stairs that held us all up in the dark red satellite threshold of bonding and chatting. I felt celestial vapor. I felt impressions of burial and resurrection. We sat on a dim lit, what I believed to be a massage table, and more. Just to my right, a couple after another couple of people began doing each-other, loving each-other, or doing something for each other on top of a swing. From dykes to men, not like the music group, Boyz II Men, this kind of chatter just beside us was a matter of passion before desire. There's levels to every course of action and the club somehow manages to give us all something that we cannot always give it, so we offer our bodies, and remember it. It is an endurance performance between dance and relation. Entry is subjective and being in it might be poetry. The quality of selection is not a vacation.

New friends feel like family, close but distant on top of those stairs. There are no mirrors. You're almost unplugged. Everything comes out. We club with the labor that provides and admits you through its doors. Everyone has their own version of it, but that should never be imposed. Everything that it takes to arrive here enters the floor. All of your life experiences throughout the years follows you to the club. Laughs cradle us to understand how our grooves become mispronounced by the outside world of obligation and social networks that often feel unreal. The club is dirt rung with nicotine smoke choking every corner of a body with sweat dripping on crooked spinal cords twisting guts to a vinyl, a queer infidelity to the nationalist charm of a country's rhythm. I fold my skin into the guts of every observer cruising my t-girl body as I would to them and promise to continue writing about death, transness, the experience of music, the black abstract, and my love for love.

The night is long. The lights are too bright till they close in on you. The darkness never diminishes, and the light is only replenishing when I realize I survived the night before. I write during the precedence of currently being in it but being in, only in the sense of making my way towards the surface. If I have to go out, please promise me that you will let me fade. When dancing, you can tell when it's your time to go, that's what service is all about, being served and serving one another. I'll leave the club of the real life in the morning when the night is not outside but inside our insides. I am no local clubgoer, I do not locate a belonging that possesses me to its place, but I must admit that it does have this visceral feeling. We take ecstasy together. I'm dancing on the edge of clarity and mystery in my words, caught in the euphoric haze of creation. I begin writing this letter near coat check. I search for no cryptic answers for the club to be what I would remember or would want it to become. I'm interested in the rise, the common belief, that we are already touching.

BLACK TRANS-FEMMES TO SONG AND DANCE

withheld means of chanting humming between lips
obliterated at work
antagonisms between scheme and schema

oblique blues imprinted elevators migratory phantoms I spiral into oblivion
inhaled into a doll

rice with some beans; the usefulness of a thing

starve out what's lost
the mystique has no ports

to tie your boats
around the bend where we've been

meeting where we've met jazz bone drills
welcome my sharks T-girls for T-girls

screaming for a make out only the parts with edges
dying before they dream bundled
in these tunnels
we cause ruckus to thought itself
where trees don't talk a thought for self

where the music just falls out of tune dead or alive. free
you can only fall when you're
off the ground

stranded on the sentiment of tongues
hung young to the sounds

across the black abstraction when life departs
a bowl for your impact
from nothing to something to hold this vacant weight, the night is long
never-more returnable forever-more etched
I wonder what signs to look for

there are no mirrors
reaching and withholding wanting to then ripple
In a distance of other bodies blisters of a paw crash

crooked spines
rugged lines waiting to fly
we club with the labor that provides and admits you through its doors.
Tgirl.jpg in rhythms

jazzing the transition
between loving the dead and recovering what's really dead you turn the knob till it
locks itself inside you
this is spiritual
this is plastic

guts spill-over like rivers rivers as children of the ocean
trans-ing the lines to Atlantic language games the upbringing of writing and contradict-
tion whither to the surround sounds of
you
that can never be unsung
to cut my throat in this hour if we make it out this dream

CURATING THE EDITING OF THE WORLD

Father Hipnosa III, a colonizer from the West and a man of faith, lived in a world where legends shaped history. Hipnosa's legacy is one of religious conviction clothed in kindness; he was certain of his own goodness because it had been passed down through the ranks of his religious order. Dressed in the robes of kindness, he found comfort in the arms of his religious beliefs, his own being becoming immersed with the holy fibers that had been enchanted by his own process of discovery.

Generations passed under the pretense of Hipnosa the 12th's care for his colonies, and from this historical shedding emerged Hipnosa the 13th, a protector of innocence and curator of the arts. All of Hipnosa's offspring are well-known to us. One day, Hipnosa crossed paths with the little and starving but fiercely artistic Black woman, Parasola. Despite being only 4'9", her popularity was so immense that it appeared to outshine even the passage of time. Hipnosa saw her only as a child, an illusion of purity and mirage of innocence. Hipnosa also referred to Parasola's grandpa and grandma, as "boy" and "chattel". Parasola had the beating heart of a 27-year-old artist who had spent time in the hallowed halls of higher education founded by Hipnosa's ancestors.

Their combined efforts resulted in a mysterious creation. An explosive bomb was Parasola's vision, a daring proclamation that may shake the foundation of Hipnosa's museum. Yet the curator's preferences leaned toward works of fantasy and spectacle. A destructive bomb that instead brings joy and forgiveness. Upon detonation, rather than sending shrapnel hurtling through the air and killing people, confetti would fall from the sky while voices pleaded with the buyers, "Acquire this art, for in its embrace lies forgiveness and reconciliation, with the promise of making America great again."

Hipnosa's legacy etched the responsibility of caretaking into the minds of future curators, who would one day take that role as their own. Black artists and other descendants of Hipnosa's colonial oppression were not immune, and some sought to become like Hipnosa themselves. Who are the protectors of culture? What price do we pay for acceptance?

WORLDING

World sleeps tight.
Fields cold, stark, and bare
Trees drip honey and roads pirouette
Rain forgets the tainted ground
Gunshots punctuate the eerie calm

Hope flickers, a candle in the shell
Dreams mumble then tell despair's
moonlit sirens and specters to dance
Over and under your head

Gunshots blend with laughter, a discordant duet
You have to run ahead
In alleys where shadows seek to form
Refuse the ground which crumbles and shatters your palms
Rain may wash the blood from stones
But can it cleanse bones?

Is that hope, or a moth? Fluttering, then still,
Frozen by the sun's whimsical seal
Misplaced heartbeats gather in puddles
Singing rebuttals of the unresolvable shuttle
Headed from one instability to another

Nowhere for scars to hide, seldom do they blend
Seldom do they survive language talking to itself

With a lump in its throat
Murmuring meaning without meaning

What's possible than the world that already is
For if world is what it is,
A welting blow of anxiety, theft, and dread
Where the young are already old enough to die
And the norm does not alternate its open eye
Then rally for that otherwise possibly
'Impossibly'

ACKNOWLEDGMENTS

Tgirl.jpg is a (re)collection of experiences made in hidden and exposed spaces where LGBTQIA+ youth shift between belonging, adulthood, and non-belonging. These spaces include trains, schools, apartments, "trips," nightclubs, and attending seminars after an all nighter from raving. *Tgirl.jpg* mirrors my own maturation and prompts a deeper inquiry into the forces that have shaped such reflections in my writing. Because of this, the experiences and perspectives of countless others have undeniably shaped this work over the past 10 years.

My return to reading poetry in 2023, after a hiatus since 2015, was spurred by Stefa Govaart's invitation. I am incredibly grateful to Stefa, but words fail me when I try to convey how important they have been to the making of this book. The editing of these poems became a conversation about the creative movement of ideas, moods, images, and offerings in a tiny New York apartment living room, as I learned the following summer from my peers and LA Warman at Warman School.

The Department of Performance Studies at NYU's Tisch School of the Arts fostered my dual pursuit of academics and artistry; for that I am incredibly appreciative. Many of the poems here were nurtured in seminars from my undergraduate days to my doctoral candidacy. Immense gratitude goes to Fred Moten, Ann Pellegrini, and André Lepecki on my committee, whose guidance continues to be invaluable to my writing practice. To my cohort Jayel Gant, Thomas (T.) Jean Lax, and George Kan, for creating an environment where we can encourage one another. Thank you to Michelle Castañeda, Malik Gaines, Diana Taylor, Barbara Browning, Alexandra T. Vazquez, Laura Elena Fortes, Avital Ronell, Pato Herbert, Karen Finley, Liana Theodoratou, and Hent De Vries. Even though I can hear their ideas in my writing, I can't think of the names for the countless others who continue to exist. I'll thank them too even if I cannot name them. Special recognition goes to the team at Free Street Theater, including Coya Paz, Katrina Dion, and Caroline O'Boyle, for nurturing my formative artistic years.

My family has been my foundation–especially my mother, Tiffany Littona Carrington, and relatives Marquis Antonio Seabron, Eliijah Malik-Lee Blanton, Danielle and De'Ja Blackwell, Brenda Calhoun, Tashanti Blanton, Cheryl and Adrian Jackson, and Jewel Carrington. To my queer guardians, Ricardo Gamboa and Sean James William Paris, your support since the Young Fugitives ensemble has been a beacon.

This book also stands on the shoulders of recent collaborators, friend-ships, and comrades in study–Leilani Douglas, Alfonzo Khalil, Zac East-erling, Juliana Fadil-Luchkiw, Nour Helou, Chip Kimura, Alia Al-Sabi, Elijah Ruiz, Alexander Rodriguez, Nína Hjálmarsdóttir, Susana MJ Kwon, Joanna Ruth Evans, Isaac Silber, Anel Rakhimzhanova, Leonor Mendes, Henry Wilcox, Eva Margarita, Amany Khalifa, and Victor Peterson II. The entire Louisiana Creole/Kouri-Vini Practice Group deserves my deepest gratitude. Finally in loving memory but never loss of memory, to Tyshawn Blanton.

ROOF BOOKS

the best in language since 1976

Recent & Selected Titles

- THE POLITICS OF HOPE (After the War) by Dubravka Djurić, translated by Biljana D. Obradović, 148 pp. $25
- SECRET SOUNDS OF PONDS by David Rothenberg, 138 pp. $29.95
- BAINBRIDGE ISLAND NOTEBOOK by Uche Nduka, 248 pp. $20
- MAMMAL by Richard Loranger, 128 pp. $20
- FOR TRAPPED THINGS by Brian Kim Stefans, 138 pp. $20
- EXCURSIVE by Elizabeth Robinson, 140 pp. $20
- I, BOOMBOX by Robert Glück, 194 pp. $20
- TRUE ACCOUNT OF TALKING TO THE 7 IN SUNNYSIDE by Paolo Javier, 192 pp. $20
- THE NIGHT BEFORE THE DAY ON WHICH by Jean Day, 118 pp. $20
- MINE ECLOGUE by Jacob Kahn, 104 pp. $20
- SCISSORWORK by Uche Nduka, 150 pp. $20
- THIEF OF HEARTS by Maxwell Owen Clark, 116 pp. $20
- DOG DAY ECONOMY by Ted Rees, 138 pp. $20
- THE NERVE EPISTLE by Sarah Riggs, 110 pp. $20
- QUANUNDRUM: [i will be your many angled thing] by Edwin Torres, 128 pp. $20
- FETAL POSITION by Holly Melgard, 110 pp. $20
- DEATH & DISASTER SERIES by Lonely Christopher, 192 pp. $20
- THE COMBUSTION CYCLE by Will Alexander, 614 pp. $25

Roof Books are distributed by **Small Press Distribution** • spdbooks.org

Roof Books are published by **Segue Foundation**
300 Bowery FL 2 • New York, NY 10012
seguefoundation.com